all for Jesus!

all for Jesus!

Wallace D. Chappell

BROADMAN PRESS / NASHVILLE, TENNESSEE

© Copyright 1975 • Broadman Press
All rights reserved

4252-31
ISBN: 0-8054-5231-1

Subject Heading: Christian life
Dewey Decimal Classification: 248.4
Library of Congress Catalog Card Number: 74-27926
Printed in the United States of America

This is dedicated to
   Ewilda and Paul
   Whitenack,
   Peggy and Henry Trotter,
   Frances and Ed Rasnake,
   Rose and Ivan Misamore,
   Irene and Charles Bolton
      who have it
         and give it.

Foreword

Wallace Chappell does not need an "imprimatur" for the publication of this book. It is a personal relationship with the Lord of which he writes and speaks. He does not lead us down hair-splitting trails of theological jungles. Wallace believes that the closer we walk with Jesus the less we become doctrine-mongers.

He just gives us Jesus and, thus, anyone who reads these messages finds that out of them comes the Christ in one man reaching out to all who read. He proclaims the importance of church renewal through the great spiritual awakening caused by the lay witness movement. As one reads, he must realize that Wallace Chappell sees the great importance of laymen and laywomen in the community of God. The silver thread throughout the entire book is a living, loving, relating, glorious Christ. It is our Christ. It is a Christ who saves, transforms, forgives, resurrects, and redeems. It is a Christ who gives us new life.

Throughout these messages, Dr. Chappell challenges us to take up the cross and keep our eyes fixed on Jesus—to get in the game of life, and the name of the game is ALL FOR JESUS! No fence riding, no complacent Christianity, no playing church, but loving Christ with all our hearts, minds, and souls. He is saying that all should be ministers of the good news and let actions speak louder and stronger than words. Time is short and the harvest is great and the redeeming workers are few.

Only one who knows a Christ like that can preach a Christ like that. But whatever he is, Wallace Chappell is nothing without his Christ and this is the supreme impression that he gives in these pages. This is what he celebrates.

So, dear friend, read and be blessed. Someone has said that the glory of books is that they are ready when we are. Therefore, my prayer, as a great friend of Wallace Chappell, is that as you prayerfully read these lines, you will be ready. For these could be the greatest hours you have ever spent.

Dr. Thomas H. Shipmon, Sr.
Prosthodontist
Memphis, Tennessee

Preface

There are two things about life in Jesus Christ. The first is that Jesus *is the life.* The Gospel of John says, "In him was life." The second is that Jesus *gives this life.* Again in John, we read, "I came that they may have life."

Since there are so many who have never experienced this Christ-life, naturally it is new for them when it becomes real. Speaking from my own experience, there has been a growing newness in my relationship to our Lord and the Christian fellowship for three reasons.

First, a close brush with death that has caused me to do much soul searching. Second, the joy of being the senior minister of a church that majors in loving. Third, the continued influence of the Lay Witness Movement which I consider the greatest program of evangelism in the United Methodist Church, and in any church, for that matter.

We have attempted, in this modest effort, to lay down some simple guidelines; elementary truths, that we believe and trust point to the new life which Christ gives and, which in turn, is all for him.

I am indebted to my secretary, Brenda Smith, for typing this manuscript and to a patient congregation that gave these messages a prayerful and loyal hearing.

WALLACE D. CHAPPELL
McKendree United Methodist Church
Nashville, Tennessee

Contents

Foreword		**vii**
Preface		**ix**
I.	**THE NEED**	**13**
1.	*The Essential Question*	**15**
2.	*Responding to the Redeemer*	**23**
II.	**THE CALL**	**31**
3.	*An Amazing Advent*	**33**
4.	*That Winsome Invitation*	**41**
III.	**THE GIFT**	**47**
5.	*When Life Is Victorious*	**49**
6.	*This Is Our Faith*	**55**
IV.	**THE GROWTH**	**61**
7.	*The Royal Request*	**63**
8.	*Christ and His Church*	**71**
V.	**THE TASK**	**79**
9.	*The Measure of Greatness*	**81**
10.	*Why People Listened to Jesus*	**89**

I.

THE NEED

THE NERD

1.
The Essential Question

Jesus said to him, "Friend, why are you here?" (Matt.
26:50, RSV).

The betrayer has acted. The soldiers have come. Jesus
has fought and won the Gethsemane struggle.

Judas now appears in the garden, along with the crowd,
to arrest our Lord. The traitor had given this signal: "The
one I kiss is your man; seize him" (Matt. 26:48, NEB).
This done, Jesus responds with the question, "Friend, why
are you here?"

It is the only question that really matters. A world in
need—multitudes in sin—lives filled with loneliness and
despair. Why are you here?

Now, in every garden, in every community, yes, in every
church there are four groups. They are the ones who answer
this question. And make no mistake about it, each of us
belongs to one of these companies.

I

There were *the betrayers*. Judas was in the garden. And
note that he was one of the Master's own twelve. He was

15

no self-appointed follower on the periphery of discipleship. He had been chosen, as the others, to be an apostle. Not only that, but he held the trusted position of treasurer (John 12:6).

The person who harms the Christian cause more than any other is not the outside critic but the *inside traitor*.

The great German preacher, Helmut Thielicke, tells of a certain man who was quite hostile to Hitler's movement. Betrayed to the Gestapo, he spent many months in concentration camps. After the war had ended, he returned to his home, not in the best of health, perhaps, but at least in control of his senses and with his head held high. Soon he found that it was his own son who had betrayed him. The man's faculties collapsed and he hanged himself. What the Third Reich could not do, knowledge that one so close had turned traitor did do, and the result was suicide.

We betray our Lord in two ways: what we do and what we fail to do. Judas betrayed by what he did. Peter, on the other hand, proved false by what he didn't do. And, mark you, Peter's denial was nearly as subversive as Judas' betrayal.

For a moment, let us look at these two methods of treachery.

First, *betrayal by action.* When Jesus outlined his cross-bearing mission, we read this grave result: "Many of his followers turned back and would not go with him any more" (John 6:66, TEV). It is a tragic fact that Calvary does turn off many would-be followers. But it is a triumphant fact that many will respond to a summons of service rather than solace. The cross is the great dividing point. We in the church are inviting people to accept either what we offer or what Christ demands.

Take a look at the difference. Our offer: cushioned pews coffee and doughnuts, elegant facilities. His demand: a cross, a ministry, world invasion. Play fair now with your heart. Which summons really makes its appeal to you?

Second, *betrayal by inaction.* There are so many points of consideration that could be made here. But betrayal speaks of those who have walked with our Lord, so let us speak briefly to this.

So often we say that our lives are our testimonies, and this is true. Your witness will count for little if you do not have a devoted life to back it up. But often God must use my telling and my doing to get his message through. Remember he placed a high premium on speaking when he said, "By your words you will be justified, and by your words you will be condemned" (Matt. 12:37, RSV).

However, it is the doing or not doing that is often the key to victorious witness.

"I would like to know," said a sarcastic, drunken playboy, "what happened to all the money my father gave to the church?"

"I would like to know," answered the minister to whom he was speaking, "what happened to all the money your father didn't give to the church."

We find ourselves constantly, both internationally and nationally, in one crisis after another. If ever the world needed churchmen, redemptive agents, who will not compromise his cause, it is now. Friend, why are you here?

II

The sleepers were in that garden—they are in every fellowship.

Jesus asked those closest to him to share his vigil in Gethsemane. Now certainly they needed him. Had they yielded to the Father's will in the garden, they would not have lost their witness temporarily after the garden. But the main reason, I think, that Jesus urged them to watch with him was because for those exceedingly difficult hours he needed them.

There is an old story about a little girl of six who became quite afraid one night during a storm. Running into her mother's room she exclaimed, "Mama, the lightning—the thunder—I'm scared." Her mother said, "Now, dear, don't be frightened. The Lord is with you." "That may be," she replied, "but I want somebody in my room with skin on him." Have we not all known times like that?

The New English Bible translates with sympathy: "He [Jesus] found them asleep, worn out by grief" (Luke 22:46). Nevertheless, it is tragically true that when our Lord was counting on them with desperate eagerness, the disciples went to sleep and thus were in no position to help.

A farmer took his little son with him one morning to be his companion while he plowed. At noon they divided a lunch as they rested under the shade of a tree. The father had admonished the child to stay away from a nearby cliff so often that he failed to warn him this particular time. Leaning back against the tree, he was almost instantly asleep. He awoke with a start sometime later and noted immediately that the boy was nowhere to be seen. Rushing to the edge of the precipice, he saw the broken body of his son far below.

Hours later as he walked beside a little white casket, close friends heard him repeat over and over: "I just went to sleep—I just went to sleep."

How the Master's broken heart longed for the strength of the disciples' companionship. And they went to sleep.

Could this possibly be the supreme tragedy of the church? Drowsy discipleship? Indifference to the brotherhood? An insensibility to the divine command, "Go and make disciples of all nations"?

I received a letter from a lady in a distant state speaking

to this spiritual wakefulness which just may be our greatest lack. Here is a part of that letter. I have not altered the wording. (Italics are mine.)

> As members of a downtown Methodist Church, my husband and I were interested in your program. We learned of the Thursday noon services, and of the Wednesday evening prayer meetings, suppers, and council meetings. We met many people and each one helped us to feel welcome.
>
> We learned of your new venture in the busing program. We saw your chapel and your fine children's facilities. We heard the music of your choir and organist. We worshiped with your people at the 11:00 service and were inspired.
>
> As interested church members, we were searching for the key to the secret that makes your people drive three or twenty miles to be a part of your fellowship.
>
> And I think we found it. I don't believe that it was the program, the staff, or the fine facilities. *I felt that your people live in a spirit of openness and friendliness that permits the entrance of the Holy Spirit to work through them and inspire them as they serve our Lord.*
>
> Such an elementary ingredient of the Christian life. Yet how often it is missing. May God bless you and your congregation as they continue in their mission.

Could there be a greater lay ministry and witness than this?

Friend, why are you here?

III

Then, there were *the arresters*. In the garden there was an armed crowd that had been sent by the chief priests and elders.

Of course, it was not the first time a group had attempted to apprehend Jesus. On another occasion an arrest was ordered and when those with this authority returned empty-handed, their only excuse was, "No man ever spoke like this man!" (John 7:46, RSV).

We always have with us those who are willing to follow the orders of others. Now I am not speaking here of the business or vocational world. Employer and employee have to maintain this relationship, and our defense system is built upon it. One of the basic problems of our nation, yes, and of our world today is the disrespect for authority—especially the right kind of authority.

I am thinking more at this point of those who are driven by others' judgments and influenced by others' guidance. We so often develop the thought patterns of our contemporaries. In some respects this is good. Christianity is seeking to imitate our Lord, and evangelism is copying the "going-out" of the brotherhood.

But even a disciple of our Lord must think his own way through to surrender and sureness and service.

I had an experience recently that was certainly not unique. However, it is a good example of the sort of thing we are describing. Preaching in a small town, I was out for an evening stroll. As I walked in front of a certain house, a dog started barking at me. Next door, another dog followed suite. Across the street another joined in. Away over in a different block, yet one more canine voiced his sentiments. And yet that first dog was the only one that knew what he was barking about. He knew someone was out for a ramble and the others were just saying, "Amen."

There are folks in the church like that. It is not proper ground for discipleship. Luke records that three men made as though they wanted to be followers of Jesus. Evidently they had been acutely conscious of his divine call and the answering dedication of many in Galilee (Luke 9:57-62).

When, however, our Lord set certain goals for commitment, we do not read that they enlisted. Consecration to Christ is more than the emotion of seeing others respond. It is the heroic yieldedness, the reckless abandonment, of one's own life to him and his cause. Friend, why are you here?

IV

Finally, *the redeemers* were in Gethsemane. They are always present, thank the Lord! Jesus was there—the essential Redeemer. Weary disciples were there—the potential redeemers.

I have never served a church that did not have Christ's redeeming people. Some were already veterans of many Christian campaigns. Some were witnesses-in-the-making; Christians under construction, as Stanley Jones used to say. Still others were waiting for the right hand and the right voice and the right way to be led into effective discipleship. But *they are there* if seen and called and used.

This is the major merit of the lay witness missions that are the strongest examples I know of church renewal today. As these devoted Christians share their love for and confidence in Jesus Christ, hundreds of thousands are saying that by God's grace they can duplicate that ministry. And they are!

It just so happens that I love my Lord and proclaim his message for that reason. Even so, in the eyes of many, I am just a "parish priest" earning my salary. But a lay person has the happy privilege, with his beautiful unprofessional approach, of revealing God in so many unsuspecting ways.

What is our mission as servants of the redemptive ministry of our Lord?

Well, of course, we are called by our Savior to function

in many ways as sons and daughters of Calvary and the empty tomb. But our Lord summed it up in this particular way: "A new commandment I give to you, that you love one another; even as I have loved you, that you also love one another. By this all men will know that you are my disciples, if you have love for one another" (John 13:34-35, RSV).

Whatever else is our assignment, we are chosen by Christ to lead men through love.

Somewhere I heard a story that moved me deeply.

A small boy went into a pet shop. "Mister," he addressed the manager, "I want to buy that puppy." The proprietor followed the pointed finger to a little crippled dog all by himself. "Son," he replied, "that pup is worthless. We're going to have him put to sleep in the next few days." "But," the would-be-owner answered, "I have saved my money just to buy that one puppy. I have been looking at him in the window every day. He's the only one I want." Once again the manager of the store explained the problem—the dog was crippled—the dog was worthless—the dog would be put to sleep. The small chap then reached down with two little hands and pulled up his trousers. The man observed two little legs enclosed in braces. "Mister," he said, "you don't know what love can do!"

Betrayers. Sleepers. Arresters. Redeemers. Friend, why are you here?

2
Responding to the Redeemer

And it came to pass, that as they went in the way, a certain man said unto him, Lord I will follow thee whithersoever thou goest.

And Jesus said unto him, Foxes have holes, and birds of the air have nests; but the Son of man hath not where to lay his head.

And he said unto another, Follow me. But he said, Lord, suffer me first to go and bury my father.

Jesus said unto him, Let the dead bury their dead: but go thou and preach the kingdom of God.

And another also said, Lord, I will follow thee: but let me first go bid them farewell, which are at home at my house.

And Jesus said unto him, No man, having put his hand to the plough, and looking back, is fit for the kingdom of God (Luke 9:57-62).

We are considering here in the first two chapters the need to follow Jesus. Sometimes it is important to learn truth from a negative standpoint, as well as a positive.

I am forever hearing ministers say we must be positive. Well, if you think Jesus was always positive, you might try reading the twenty-third chapter of Matthew or the twelfth chapter of Mark or the sixteenth chapter of Luke. And though we enjoy being rapturous about the thirteenth chapter of 1 Corinthians—Paul's great love letter—it is interesting to note he goes into great detail about what love is not. And when we get right down to it, the majority of the Ten Commandments are negative.

The call of the Master goes out to three different men. Here are their responses:

"Lord, I will follow thee whithersoever thou goest," (until Jesus outlines the difficulties of discipleship).

"Lord, suffer me first to go and bury my father."

"Lord, I will follow thee; but let me first go bid them farewell, which are at home at my house."

Let us consider each of these.

I

The first man's response, *an unconquered fear.* "I will follow you (he seems to say), but . . . ." This man sounds so much like Peter. Listen to the fisherman, "Lord, I am ready to go with thee, both into prison, and to death." But, evidently, the high priest's house was a more difficult place of witness than a cell or a cross, for Simon failed miserably in the hour of need. Indeed, this first opportunity was a cross that Peter neglected to take.

"Foxes have holes," said Jesus, "and birds have nests. The Son of man hath not where to lay his head."

After hearing these words from the lips of our Lord, this would-be-follower was never heard from again. Make no mistake about it—unless one is ready to surrender everything to Jesus Christ and his cause, homeless discipleship offers little appeal. He was afraid. But that was not the tragedy. Here was his besetting sin: He did not trust the Master with his fear.

Sometime ago I was attempting to sail through treacherous waters. A letter from a dear saint in our fellowship made all the difference. She wrote her pastor these words. "Always remember that Jesus only asks one thing—that we trust him." How meaningful to have a lay person share with her minister like that!

Now Christ's call to enlistment without ease did not make this particular man a coward. It simply revealed the uncommitted cowardice that was existent in his life.

I once heard about a young man who escorted his fiancee to a motion picture theater. In the middle of the movie, someone suddenly shouted, "Fire!" Off he ran with great speed. When he got out about the marquee, he discovered that he was running alone and that there had been a false alarm. Returning to his seat with a sackcloth and ashes appearance, he said, "Excuse me." And she did—permanently.

The point is, however, it was not the embarrassing event that made him a coward. It simply proved him a coward. The fact was disclosed that basic within his nature was the potential to be spineless.

So this man came to Jesus with such halfhearted allegiance that he was frightened, not by the first sign of conflict, but by the mere mention of privation. How easily did he become a Christian drop-out. In fact, he never dropped in.

When I was in high school, I ran on the track team. I remember in one meet being disqualified for twice jumping the gun. Now it was bad to lose a race by just a step. But it was more embarrassing to lose when you had never started.

How easily did this latent recruit allow himself to be removed from the potential scene of service. He was like the cowardly lion in the motion picture version of *The Wizard of Oz*. Realizing that Dorothy was a prisoner and that someone should release her from the power of the wicked witch, he was all ready to start out on this venture. He asked only one thing of the scarecrow and tin man. "Talk me out of it," was his request.

Christ's potential disciple was talked out of it because he failed to surrender his fear.

II

The second man's response was, "Lord, suffer me first to go and bury my father." If the first man's problem was an unconquered fear, the second man's difficulty was an *unburied father.*

I am thinking of an elderly country preacher who used to add this sentence to the man's reply: "And I'll just bet his old daddy wasn't even sick."

My guess is that this particular person was simply not being truthful. This has to be the case in the light of our Lord's reaction to his response. Jesus never would have been so heartless as to have said what he did in the light of a broken heart where death had come. The chances are very strong that Jesus spent much more time taking care of his family than he did initiating a kingdom. (If Joseph did in fact die while Jesus was quite young as legend suggests, then as the elder brother and one in charge, he spent many more years in service in his home than out in the fields as an itinerant preacher.)

This being the case, we have here an excuse and not a reason, and there is a world of difference between the two. A reason has foundation and an excuse may have fabrication and it was to this particular that our Lord addressed himself. Until our Lord can get a man to face reality, he can never get him to radiant discipleship.

The great philosopher, Alfred North Whitehead, was dead right when he affirmed, "Look for truth and you will run straight into Jesus Christ." The best thing about Bishop Robinson's provocative publication, *Honest to God,* is not the book, but the title. Whatever else is included in commitment to our Lord there must be the oldest virtue of all—honesty.

I remember once in a former parish a young woman, who was a member of our church and also a close friend of our family, requesting a counseling period.

When she walked in my study, I could tell she was at odds with the world in general and the Christian fellowship in particular. "I want my name removed from the church roll," she said and proceeded to spout off what she considered her reasons.

Feeling that it would do little good to argue, I suggested a prescription that I learned from a physician. "Take fifteen minutes each morning for a week," I urged. "Spend five minutes reading the Bible—five minutes thinking about what you have read—five minutes speaking with the Lord. When you have completed the week, come back and we'll talk about dropping your name from our membership roll."

She completed that week and she completed many weeks in a similar fashion for she recently graduated from our church-related college, Scarritt, and is an active and constant worker in her church.

Thus facing the truth prayerfully, she is now facing her tasks victoriously.

III

The third man's response was *an unyielded heart.* "I will follow thee," he says, "but . . . first . . . (let me) bid them farewell which are at my home."

In his very fine little book, *The Promise of the Spirit,* William Barclay says, "One of the unmistakable features of [the book] Acts is the way in which it tells us that every great decision which the Church took was taken under the guidance of the Spirit."

This man in the Gospel of Luke says, "First, let me say good-bye to my people at home."

Jesus says in this same Gospel, "If any man will come after me, let him deny himself, and take up his cross daily and follow me" (Luke 9:23, KJV).

There is no question as to what is paramount. It is no puzzle as to what must come first. The man said, "First, let me." Jesus said, "First, follow me." This is where it happens. To be sure other things must come along: the growing—the learning—the sharing. But, *the following!* That's what makes a brand-new ball game!

And notice: It was the most precious thing in his life that was serving as barrier, his family. We spoke in the last point of Jesus' care for his own. But there came a time in our Master's life when he had to leave even the sanctity of his home for service in the world.

Our Lord's summons, then, is always an appeal to the present. An entreaty to the immediate. A call to the now. First! First! First! And there were simply other things that counted more to this man than the cause of Christ. The unyielded heart—that is the greatest barrier to belonging.

I heard a story once about a young girl who was warned by her mother that dinner time was near and she must stay out of the pantry.

The little girl, however, was less interested in spoiling her appetite than in eating sweets. Her mother caught her slipping out of the pantry with one little hand clenched tightly behind her back. Opening the child's fingers, the mother found a little marshmallow buried in her palm.

The lady telling the story then asked, "Is there anything you are keeping from God—just what is your marshmallow?"

I told that story to my congregation recently and one of our lovely soprano soloists came to the altar. When I asked her why she had come, she answered simply, "To give my last marshmallow to Christ."

Three men in the long ago had their chance and rejected it. This could be for you a significant spiritual hour. Don't miss it!

II.

THE CALL

3.
An Amazing Advent

> He went up and touched the bier. Those who were
> carrying it stood still. "Young man," He said, "I tell you,
> rise!" (Luke 7:14, Barclay).

In the first two chapters we considered the need for Jesus.
We turn now to the call of Jesus.

However, one must note that you cannot divorce the
invitation from the Inviter, the summons from the Savior;
the call from the Christ.

One follows immediately. Always, if Christianity is to
be the life-giving power that it was for the daring disciples
of New Testament times, the Christ must lead directly to
the claim.

Here in the village of Nain we see this illustrated to
perfection. This is the situation in capsule.

The problem: death

The presence: Jesus

The pinnacle: life

And it is right here at this point that we see his amazing
advent. That a Messiah would come to destroy Rome, well
now that was believable—that was anticipated—that was
desired. But a Galilean carpenter—an itinerant preacher—a

humble servant—that was something else.

Again, it was not difficult to hope for a Redeemer bringing vengeance and destruction and judgment. But one speaking of forgiveness—teaching of love—the sharing of life! You see that was a different thing.

Yet it was to give life that he came and he said so (John 10:10).

In this story, then, we visualize his amazing advent; his coming to give life.

I

His amazing advent; this coming to give life, was a *personal* demonstration. This was not a miracle by proxy. Not only so, but it was not done from a distance. In this same chapter, Jesus had healed a Roman centurion's servant, but it was by faith and not sight.

At Nain, however, Jesus was visibly present. Notice, too, he directs his remarks straight to the boy who had died: "Young man," he says. Luke may even have left something out. Perhaps Jesus had learned his name and addressed him in that respect. It would have been like Mark to have inserted that. Be that as it may, it was a deeply personal experience. We read, for instance, that Jesus walked over to the coffin and actually touched it (v. 14).

There is absolutely no substitute for this personal element of which we speak. Luther was right when he observed that religion must major in that element. Of course, I would plug for its validity in any area.

My friend, Harry Denman, told me of something that backs up this statement. A young man went away to graduate school leaving his sweetheart behind. They planned to be married a year hence. Each day during the year he wrote her a note assuring her of his love and intention to marry her. Dr. Denman climaxed the story in his own abrupt manner with this brutally frank sentence: "At the end of the year she married all right but she married the mailman—its the personal touch that counts."

Well, we can laugh at this incident (which Brother Harry declares is factual), but the truth that it suggests is no laughing matter.

Jesus went personally to Galilee and personally to Nain and personally to a casket and called a boy back to life.

The church of the living God must realize today that the personal touch is its task. Our twentieth-century world demands it. People come seeking fellowship in the church, the body of Christ, only when that body has extended itself in an intimate outreach to their door. It is the person who is made to feel special that harbors the hope for the spiritual. The cause of evangelism can only be won when we enable people to see that every person is important to Christ.

Just recently I was explaining to a mother why I felt it urgent to visit her daughter and son-in-law. They were preparing to transfer their membership. Later that week in the actual setting of the home, the communication and prayer and dedication (for it was in fact much more than simply a transfer) led me to say this to that mother. "There are some things that just can't happen over the telephone or through the postal service."

II

If his amazing advent was personal at this point, it was also *authoritative*. "I tell you—Rise up!" he said. Now that's not a suggestion. That's a command!

Of course, it was in this spirit that our Lord always spoke and acted. Early in his ministry it was this particular that brought astonishment to the multitudes for "he taught as one who had great authority, and not as their Jewish leaders!" (Matt. 7:29, TLB). The scribes repeated—Jesus professed. The scribes transcribed—Jesus affirmed. The scribes copied—Jesus declared.

Observe also to whom Jesus was addressing this command. He was literally ordering a dead man to return to life. So! His authority prevails not only over life but over death!

Nor is this the only incident in the New Testament that gives credence to this statement. In the Gospel of Mark we find our Lord saying, "Little girl, rise, I tell you" (5:41, Moffatt). And in the Gospel of John, we hear his word, "Lazarus, come out!" (11:43, Moffatt).

Now, the question before the house is where does he need to speak with authority in your life and mine? What is that dead area that needs his life-giving presence? Where does his amazing advent need to take place in our lives?

Here is a man who is betraying his wife. He isn't happy about it but, in his own strength, he does not have the stamina to return to fidelity. He, as well as the one who tempts him, can only walk that road under the authority of Christ.

Here is a college student and the drug habit has him. By himself he is powerless to break the almost invincible chains that bind him. Christ alone has the authority to bring such freedom.

Here is a church member. So long has he played church instead of being Christian that he scarcely recognizes the difference between counterfeit and consecration. He needs the authority of Christ to bring him to dynamic reality.

We possess the potential—it lies within each of our hearts. He has the power and he yearns to exercise that authority upon us.

The incomparable W. E. Sangster, so many years minister of Westminster Hall, London, was one of my preaching heroes.

While he was still a young minister, he heard about a great spiritual awakening sweeping a certain city. Sangster went to that city to investigate the rumors of victorious renewal. Approaching a policeman he asked, "Where is the religious revival taking place?" The answer was immediate. "Under these buttons, laddie, under these buttons."

And our Lord can give us that spirit of triumph. He only has the authority!

III

The personal. The authoritative. Finally, our Lord's amazing advent at Nain was *compassionate*.

How tremendously important is this! In fact there is nothing quite so urgent. Of the eternal values, Paul says, the greatest is love (1 Cor. 13:13).

But, to be sure, the supreme revealer of this essential is our blessed Lord himself. Mark describes that fact in these poignant words: "He saw a great crowd; and his heart went out to them, because they were like sheep without a shepherd" (Mark 6:34, NEB). Oh! The compassion of Christ!

Sometime ago I was flying to another city for a preaching engagement. On our plane was a young girl whose mother had painfully and patiently prepared her for the flight. She wore her grandmother's name and address tied to her sleeve. She was retarded.

Seldom have I been more deeply moved as I watched the concern of the two stewardesses on duty for that precious handicapped child. They gave her more ministry than I have given members of my congregation in areas where I have served for years. You see, they cared.

Again this is the greatest merit of the lay witness mission: sharing because of caring.

It was our Lord's care that involved him in Nain. He was deeply concerned with the distressed mother. Certainly he was sorry about the young man's death, but his suffering, if there was any, had ended. The mother's pain was just beginning: the pain of grief and loneliness and despair. Luke says, "When the Lord saw her, his heart overflowed with sympathy" (7:13, TLB).

He then left her and walked to the coffin and called the lad back to life.

My friend, John Porter, who was a chaplain in Vietnam, received a letter once that had great meaning for me. Here is a copy:

DEAR CHAPLIN,

I ain't much with words and I get a little tongue-tied when I try to say what I mean about something that's really important. I'd like to say this to you face-to-face, but maybe I can do it better in a letter. First off, you know the kind of guy I've been. . . . I'm not gonna try to hide that. Everybody in the unit knows ole Gus, the big man, that's what I've tried to be. I guess I've fooled about everybody. The only thing really big about me has been my bluff. But, Chaplin, you and God saw through me and you made me see myself, and what I saw made me sick. You showed me one thing. I talked a lot about the hell of Vietnam. It was in me. I didn't find it over here; I brought it with me. Chaplin, I don't know how to pray, but last night I told God to count me in. I've been such a slob I didn't want to ask a regular preacher like you to baptize me, so when nobody was watching I baptized myself in the creek. When I prove that I ain't kidding about all this, I want you to do it again the way it should be done.

A member on God's team,
Gus

And Chaplain Porter added, "Before the letter reached me, Gus had been killed."

It was the chaplain's compassion that made new life possible for Gus. It was Jesus' compassion that gave new life to the boy. Are you and I sharing God's new life with others?

4.
That Winsome Invitation

> Come to me, all who labor and are heavy laden, and I will give you rest. Take my yoke upon you, and learn from me; for I am gentle and lowly in heart, and you will find rest for your souls. For my yoke is easy, and my burden is light (Matt. 11:28-30, RSV).

In considering the call of Jesus, we look to this particular Scripture as the most radiant of all his requests.

However, before we examine these marvelous words, there are two observations, I feel, that are worth noting.

The first is that I am definitely prejudiced as I comment on this great theme from Matthew's Gospel. This Scripture is my favorite in all the Bible. When the skies have been sunny, I have come to these words. And when the day has been bleak and the night has been lonely, I have sought refuge in the gentle embrace of its tender arms.

The second observation is this: The things that have been most beneficial and blessed in my life and ministry have happened as I responded to meaningful invitations.

Just before I became nineteen, I went one evening to a residential church in Birmingham to hear a man named Edwin Holt Hughes preach on "The Romance of the Ministry." My life was entirely changed because of the invitation he extended that evening.

While still in seminary, I was invited by a minister to preach in a lovely little Virginia town. I met a girl that week, and later she became mistress of the manse. A rare splendor was added by her presence and I know what Elizabeth Barrett Browning meant when she wrote,

> The face of all the world is changed, I think,
> Since first I heard the footsteps of thy love.

Then, I was endeavoring to serve a Methodist appointment; a four-point circuit in the hills of east Tennessee when I received a long-distance call from the resident bishop of the Nashville area. It was an invitation to become pastor of a church where because of his Spirit doors opened and lives changed.

But here is the greatest of all invitations I know: "Come to me, all who labor and are heavy laden, and I will give you rest. Take my yoke upon you, and learn from me; for I am gentle and lowly in heart, and you will find rest for your souls. For my yoke is easy, and my burden is light" (Matt. 11:28-30, RSV).

I

Look first at the words, "Come to me," and consider *the Lord.*

Notice, he did not say come to the Temple or come to the synagogue or even come to the fellowship of the disciples. He said, "Come to me."

Emerson never spoke more wisely than when he observed that an institution was the lengthened shadow of one man. This is especially true in the light of our Christian faith. The greatest need is not for a dogma but a Deliverer, not a maxim but a Master, not a creed but a Christ!

This is where we miss religion at its radiant best. For Aristotle, God was a process. For Jesus, God was a person. My friend, Fred Speakman, says we believe in God because he had a Galilean face.

But oh! The substitutes we make. Like Aristotle we delve into processes or other unsatisfying invitations. We go to money or prestige or drugs or sex or even church duties sometimes. Jesus saw this during his earthly ministry. Read again his words to those seeking meaning in the wrong places: "You are not willing to come to me in order to have life" (John 5:40, TEV). As our current youthful generation quips, "That's where it's at."

II

Then our Lord says, "all who labor and are heavy laden." Consider *the load.* Many of the people in the time of Jesus were bearing heavy burdens—many are today.

There are some, for instance, whose work is sheer dread. During my ministry, both in country and city, I have seen people who labored until the weight of their work was an almost impossible encumbrance.

I doubt if America has ever had a greater singer than Marian Anderson. She was asked, once, what was the supreme moment of her life. How many answers she could have given—this woman who sang before the nobility of Europe and the leadership of America—but her response was beautifully simple. "The greatest moment in my life," she replied, "was when I received enough money from singing that I could tell my mother she no longer had to take in washing."

Then, sadness is a heavy burden. When the disciples went to sleep in the garden, *The New English Bible* justifies their conduct with these words: "He found them . . . worn out by grief" (Luke 22:46). That does make a difference!

With this mood I can identify. I recently took a three hundred and fifty mile death journey that involved one quite close to me, and the burden seemed heavier at times than I could bear.

Hate is a burden. What a tremendous ball and chain this is about a person's neck and heart. And it is dead weight we need not bear for our Lord can remove it. His promise in the twenty-eighth verse encompasses every need.

A man makes a pretty strong commitment when he can say:

> I have closed the door on hate—
>   He comes only to deceive and destroy.
> Love will come if I but wait
> For some deed of mercy I can do,
> And hate can't live where love is true—
>   And that is the cause of joy!

A friend, who is a layman, shared with me recently an experience he declared had changed his life. And it had! He was a man from the deep South and had wrestled for years with prejudice. "Wallace," he said ecstatically, "I have laid my intolerence on the altar. I have put my hate in the hands of Christ. I am free." Then he added with a grin, "Would you believe I just sat down and wrote Hank Aaron and told him I hoped he would break Babe Ruth's home run record?"

Finally, unforgiven sin is, in my opinion, the heaviest load of all. This is the burden we do not yield—the unrepentant heart we do not surrender.

A man committed suicide recently and left a note giving a single line reason: "I can't live with myself any more." But this very invitation in Matthew's Gospel tells of a companionship that can see us through any yesterday of regret, any today of loneliness, any tomorrow of fear.

III

Jesus said, "I will give you rest." At this point we think of *the lift.*

It used to be that I rather looked with disdain on the word "Comforter," which is the Authorized Version's translation for the Holy Spirit. I felt it was rather a weak word—a soft interpretation. I was far afield. It is always so easy to think something right by observation and then find it wrong by experience. It is a word with power and energy and grace. This has recently been proved to me as I have walked through the shadows and found adequate power for that journey. The truth of the matter is that he, the Holy Spirit, himself, is everything powerful and energizing and grace-giving. Or, as Bonhoeffer succinctly states it, "He not only has a word but is the Word."

So! It is his very presence that lifts us regardless of the burden. "I will give you rest," but the resting is the raising.

Once a couple was passing through deep waters. Their anguish was great. Their pastor came to see them and attempted to offer consolation.

He read that sublime promise from Deuteronomy: "The eternal God is thy refuge, and underneath are the everlasting arms" (Deut. 33:27, KJV).

Yet, when the minister left, he felt he had failed to offer effectual help. Suddenly, and I am certain it was because the dear Spirit was speaking to him, he turned around and ran back to the distraught home. "I did not give his word the emphasis I should have," he said to the husband and wife. "The arms of God are not up there flapping around in the sky somewhere—they are *underneath!* They are *underneath!*"

IV

"Take my yoke upon you." Look, finally, at *the life.*

We are companioned by Christ; "yokefellows," as Elton Trueblood has it.

A yoke is a wooden frame that joins oxen for the purpose of moving a load. Here in the Gospel of Matthew we are yoked with Jesus Christ for the purpose of changing the world.

Yet, let us always remember that it is through his grace, and because of his power, and with his presence that the new life in our Lord is shared. We are, in fact, yoked with him but may we never forget Leslie Weatherhead's significant word that "the Savior carries the heavy end."

The call of Christ is ever an invitation to walk with him. He never says go until he says come. Through us he wants to call all people to be his disciples of truth—his friends of faith—his companions of love.

Think of it! We are to live and love and lift with him, hand in hand and heart in heart as we go on the divine conquest—the sharing of his good news with humanity. It is this that marks the supreme strength of the lay witness mission.

James Stewart, in my opinion the prince of preachers, reaches a great moment in one of his books. In *Heralds of God* he tells of a letter that was written by a commander of a British ship, an officer who sailed under Lord Nelson. Pointing out the calamities through which they were passing, the commander wrote, "We are half-starved, and otherwise inconvenienced by being so long out of port. But our reward is—we are with Nelson!"

I know a greater glory. It is the eternal joy of being yokefellows with our Redeemer. We are with Christ!

III.

THE GIFT

5.
When Life Is Victorious

Fear not, little flock; for it is your Father's good pleasure
to give you the kingdom (Luke 12:32, RSV).

We have thought about the need and the call. We turn
now to the gift.

There are few texts in the Bible that speak, I think, to
joyless hearts like this word from the Gospel of Luke. And
make no mistake about it, there is much amusement in
our world, much shoddy laughter—a lot of instant fun and
sudden thrills that turn into *wreck*reation—but real joy?
I wonder.

And is this God-experience called joy a winsome reality
even in his church? Do those of us who seek to lead others
to the fellowship eternal show them the actuality of our
Lord by the glow on our faces which springs from the
assurance in our hearts?

"Joy," said Teilhard de Chardin, "is the most infallible
sign of the presence of God." Is this true? And, if it is,
are we getting the message across?

A retired minister in another area paid me a compliment
some time ago that I certainly did not deserve. Never-

theless, it was a meaningful commendation that I have been trying to strive after.

He came in the sanctuary where I was preaching and occupied a front seat. Quite elderly, he was also very deaf and heard but little of what I said. After a noon service, he accosted me and enveloped me in his arms.

"Wallace," he said huskily, "you sure did look a good sermon today." As I have already indicated, I did not feel worthy of this gracious expression. But I did get alone with the Lord after my dear friend had left. In my secret closet I prayed that Christ would help me prove with joy his kind word of approbation.

But, if you want a fresh and lifting and gladsome bit of news from heaven, what about this refreshing utterance: "Fear not, little flock: for it is your Father's good pleasure to give you the kingdom." Now, why is this such a joyous word?

I

This great statement from the lips of our Lord that fills us with joy and points us to victorious living first of all gives us *courage:* "Fear not."

It is important to note, however, that courage is not something which is individually initiated. For the Christian courage is not put on or drummed up or self-imposed. It is God-given.

And it is also necessary that we realize God gives courage because we give him confidence. Soul-strength and heart-help come to us because we believe and have faith that God can, in fact, present this gift to us.

Do you recall how that president of the synagogue, Jairus, by name, came to Jesus with a desperate need?

"My little daughter lieth at the point of death," he said

"I pray thee, come and lay thy hands on her, that she may be healed." And that great heart that has yet to turn the first man down went with him to his house.

When they arrived, the professional mourners were going all out. It is interesting to observe how quickly their tears turned into laughter when Jesus pronounced that "the damsel is not dead but sleepeth." I think it says something about their sympathy.

Nevertheless, our Lord said to Jairus, "Be not afraid, only believe." And, you know, this changed my whole philosophy about bravery. I had always thought that the opposite of fear was courage, but Jesus reveals to us that the opposite of fear is faith. And when we have faith in him, the courage comes. It came to Jairus and the victory was his. To be sure, then, the little girl was cured. However, even as she was cured of her illness, her father was cured of his cowardice. And perhaps this triumph of faith was an even greater glory.

It might be wise to add one further point. Mark's Gospel says that "he [Jesus] taketh the father and the mother of the damsel . . . and entereth in where the damsel was lying" (Mark 5:40). So! The courage Christ gives is the courage to go on, to follow through, to face danger.

It is not the absence of difficulty. Courage is the facing of fear in the companionship of the Master.

On the eve of a battle, someone said to Old Hickory, "General Jackson, your knees are shaking." He replied, "They would shake a lot more if they knew where I was fixing to take them in the next thirty minutes."

Jairus went in the room where his daughter was ill. *But he went in with Jesus.*

And we can walk into any room, face any danger, endure any trial if we journey in Christ's presence.

II

The second word is implied in the phrase, "little flock." That is to say, He gives us his *shepherding influence.*

I really do not know a word which describes our Lord, and speaks to my heart, like the word "shepherd."

Speaking to that lovely verse in the Gospel of John: "I am the good shepherd, and know my sheep" (John 10:14), Leslie Weatherhead has a memorable question. He says, "Christ is willing to say *my sheep* about you—are you willing to say *my shepherd* about him?"

Our shepherd yearns to be the leader of every flock; he is our shepherd, we are his sheep. That is a pastor-people relationship, and it should be one of great beauty and significant meaning.

Now it so happens that I love to preach. I always preach at least three sermons each week in my parish and sometimes five or six. In addition, my people allow me to be away in missions and conferences, perhaps too often. But they are beautifully unselfish.

Yet, though I seek to give preparation and delivery of sermons a paramount place in my ministry, I know of nothing so important as being a pastor to the people who need a loving guide and a tender hand and a shepherd heart. Though some may disagree, I, for one, am convinced that the pulpit is but an extension of the itinerant road over which the shepherd is seeking to guide the lambs.

There are many reasons I could give for this statement. Let one suffice. Things happened in Jesus' ministry in homes (Peter's mother-in-law being healed, for instance) that never happened in large encounters. I can speak to this reality, also.

One night I felt impressed to go to a certain home and share my witness with a family. However, I had been there a number of times, and did not particularly want to go. But the impression persisted so I called on the telephone and spoke briefly with the wife. Her response was anything but enthusiastic, although she granted permission for her pastor to visit.

An hour later she met me at the front door, greeting me with warmth and welcome. We scarcely sat down before she handed me the suicide note. It was to be that night and she is not an emotional actress. Then she handed me a bottle with two hundred and fifty phenobarbital.

"Just knowing somebody cared," she said, "has made all the difference."

Would to God I had always been as faithful to my Lord's guidance and my people's needs.

III

Christ gives us his courage: "Fear not." Christ gives us his shepherding influence: "Little flock." Finally, Christ gives us his *kingdom:* "It is your Father's good pleasure to give you the kingdom."

When Jesus speaks of the kingdom in the Gospels, he has three things in mind.

First, he means the rule of God in the world. This is that for which we pray when, in the Lord's Prayer, we say, "Thy kingdom come."

Second, he means the afterlife. This was Jesus' intention that night in the upper room when he said, "I will not drink henceforth of this fruit of the vine, until that day when I drink it new with you in my Father's kingdom."

The rule of God in the world, the blessing of God in heaven, and now the life of God in the heart: "It is your Father's good pleasure to give you the kingdom."

Elmo has always been one of my favorite characters in the comics. Do you remember when he approached Dagwood and informed him he had a new television? But when he brought his hand from behind his back, Dagwood saw that he held only a very poor substitute.

"Elmo," he said, "that's not a television—that's just a shoe box with a hole in it."

"Oh, but Mr. Bumstead," replied Elmo, "it hasn't been turned on yet."

I am thinking of a certain civic leader. At present, his only interest is making money and gaining a reputation. When God becomes real in this man's life, there is little telling how far his influence will reach as he gives his witness to other businessmen. You say you don't see that? But he hasn't been turned on yet!

There is a lovely socialite in our city. Today her main concerns are cocktail parties and bridge clubs. When Jesus is given first place in her heart, the radiance of her consecration will go through silky suburbia like the sunshine. You say you don't see that? But she hasn't been turned on yet!

Struggling teenagers are everywhere in our parish. They are being tempted every day by drugs and alcohol and sex. When the Holy Spirit enters, he will give a glorious reason for loving and a contagious gladness in sharing it. You say you don't see that? But they haven't been turned on yet!

The kingdom in this context means the life of God in the heart. That is what it means to be turned on. But only Christ can turn us on with his love and then turn us loose in his world. As ministers are we willing to go on his pilgrimage? As laymen are we willing to serve in his mission?

6.
This Is Our Faith

> For God so loved the world, that he gave his only begotten
> Son, that whosoever believeth in him should not perish,
> but have everlasting life (John 3:16).

I once heard about a homeless boy who drifted into
a certain town and found his acquaintances in the riffraff
of the community.

A convert of a mission passed—one who had been gen-
uinely reclaimed—saw the lad and recognized him as a
stranger in the area. Not wanting the boy to fall into
harmful habits, the man directed him to the mission where
he had found new life.

"Just tell the people John 3:16 when they come to the
door," he advised.

The lad went and found understanding and compassion.
This was expressed by a tub of warm water, a plate filled
with food, and a bed for the night. Too, a generous portion
of love attended these practical ministries.

The following day, as he journeyed looking for a job,
he met some friends of the day before. This time it was
his turn to be a sharer.

"Everything is different because of John 3:16," he said.

"We heard that man tell you those words yesterday," was the response. "What does it mean?"

"Well, you know," he answered, "I'm not quite sure what it means. But it makes a dirty person clean and a hungry person full and a tired person strong."

You can't put it under a microscope and get scientific evidence—God is not an object of study but a revelation of the soul. I only know, as the lad, that years ago I found, for a fact, that John 3:16 does make for purity and fulfillment and strength.

The gospel in miniature—that was what Martin Luther called it. Let us look briefly at this great gospel.

I

We are told in the first place, about *a great love.* "God so loved." As important as our love is, it is not the good news. The First Epistle of John relates it: "Herein is love, not that we loved God, but that he loved us" (4:10, KJV).

Somehow in our witness the people must see that this is the way the Father relates to us—not through wrath but love.

This pertinent truth was being spoken by Jesus to Nicodemus. Here was a man well qualified in religious beliefs and observances. I doubt if there was a Jew who was more adept in the Law. Yet, he was missing the gospel. So he came one night truth-thirsty, soul-seeking, and heart-hungry to the young Galilean, conscious that in him he had seen the difference between life and Life. And Jesus spoke to him, not about his love for God, but God's love for him—and the world.

That night was the start of the spread of this miniature gospel that would redeem literally millions. An intimate interview that would become a world witness!

It continues today! "God loves you." That is our great good news. That is the key word of the lay witness mission. Not enough to simply say God is love. Often when my day has been quite burdensome, my dear wife will meet me at the door with a most amazing understanding and affection. But I have never heard her greet me with, "Marriage is love." When she says, "I love you," however, the mercury in my heart-thermometer does a rapid rise.

God loves you—God loves the world. What marvelous tidings with which to begin the divine invasion!

II

God so loved the world "that he gave." Let us now look at *a great gift*.

It is imperative, I think, for us to see that our salvation, and ultimately the salvation of the world, does not depend upon the effort we exert but the gift we receive. Redemption itself must come to us not as the basis of that which we achieve but that which we accept.

I remember once that a friend offered me a present. When he noticed that I was a bit reluctant to take it, he said something that I have not forgotten. Not only so, but I have used those same words many times across the years.

"Keep in mind," he admonished, "that it is just as Christian to accept a gift as it is to give one."

Of course he was dead right. Oftentimes it is more Christian. In fact, I am insisting at this point that basic Christianity begins here.

Many years ago I read a great sermon by Harry Emerson Fosdick entitled, "Hospitality to the Highest." I have not refreshed my memory recently with the reading of that masterpiece, but I can still recall the chief consideration. Fosdick insisted that the mountain moments of his pilgrimage were in direct proportion to the vital experiences of life to which he had been hospitable and shown welcome.

"God so loved that he gave." There are many things that I can do with this gift. I can use it. I can nurture it. I can share it. But the first thing I must do is take it.

III

"That whosoever"—this speaks of *a great inclusion.*

When our Lord was presenting the parables of the kingdom, he said, "The kingdom of heaven is like unto a net, that was cast into the sea, and gathered of every kind" (Matt. 13:47, KJV).

You see, this means everybody. This is precisely what Jesus was saying in the text: God so loved the *world*—not the Jews, not the church, not the disciples—the world!

There is the old story of the woman in Scotland who came to the altar when the Lord's Supper was being served. It had been so long since she had been to her "wee Kirk" and she had known years of dissipation and heartbreak. Nevertheless, she knelt with the others when the invitation was given. As she reached out for the bread and the cup, perhaps her soiled hands and stained life whispered to her to draw back. Her minister sensed her feeling and her need.

"Take it, dear sister," he whispered tenderly, "take it, it's for sinners."

Listen again to these words: "Him that cometh to me I will in no wise cast out" (John 6:37, KJV). Let me say what blessed hope those words offer me personally. They simply mean anybody can come and the gracious Savior will receive them.

IV

We turn now to the fourth word, "believeth," and we

think of *a great requirement.*

What exactly did Jesus mean here when he spoke of belief? Most of the time when we think of believing, we associate it with mental perception. I think at this point, however, that our Lord was speaking of the concentration of the heart. Some believe and enter by way of the impact God makes on their minds. It is my conviction that most belong and enter by way of God's influence on their hearts. Nicodemus was a believer or he would not have made his night visit. Christ wanted him to be a belonger and share his faith in broad daylight.

I am not frowning on the consideration of the head. I am simply saying it is not as urgent as the confidence of the heart.

Take, for instance, that frustrated father who came with his demon-possessed son to Jesus.

"Have mercy," he appealed to the Lord. "Do something if you can."

"If I can!" was our Lord's reply. "Anything is possible if you have faith." That is, Jesus was saying, "If you will give me your heart confidence, I will give you a healed son."

And that confidence means that there is nothing held back. We are coming to him with our all.

A man with whom I had been sharing the faith came once to an evening worship service. As we were singing the last hymn, I did something I seldom do. Walking to his seat, I placed my arm around him and said, "Guy, you and I have spoken about this matter of being Christian many times. Don't you think you're ready to act on it?" His answer surprised me. "Wallace," he said, "I hear so many people say so many different things. What did Jesus really mean when he said, 'You must be born again'?"

I am certain that the dear Savior gave me the right

answer. "Guy," I replied, "when I come home at night I hold out my arms to receive my little girl. She doesn't fight or resist me—she simply rests her weight in her father's arms. That, I think, is the new birth. Will you rest your weight in the Master's arms?" And he did.

V

Finally, we look at the phrase "should not perish but have everlasting life." We have *a great destiny.*

Jesus said to the heartbroken Martha after the death of her brother, "Whosoever liveth and believeth in me shall never die." Some will answer that this is simply not true. They have in fact been beside a loved one and have watched death come. What could Jesus have meant by the words, they ask.

Our Lord said to the dying thief, "Today shalt thou be with me in paradise."

This must mean that the moment life ends here it begins somewhere else—with Christ! In order for these words "shall never die" to be valid it means that death is the door which opens to his continuing companionship. It was Jesus himself who said, "This is life eternal, that they might know thee the only true God, and Jesus Christ, whom thou hast sent" (John 17:3). So! Eternity is two things: a life that never ends and a love that never fails.

The Charles Kingsleys had a radiant marriage. Here is the epitaph he composed which speaks to this resurrection reality:

Amavimus, Amamus, Amabimus. It means from the Latin, "We loved, we love, we shall love."

What a gospel!

IV.

THE GROWTH

IV.

THE GROWTH

7.
The Royal Request

He was praying in a certain place, and when he ceased,
one of his disciples said to him, "Lord, teach us to pray,
as John taught his disciples (Luke 11:1, RSV).

We have looked at the need and the call and the gift.
We come now to consider the growth that we must antici-
pate and appropriate as Christian disciples.

This entire series deals with the Word. Too, we would
hope that witness has constantly been stressed. So as we
think of Christian development, we want to think especially
of prayer and the gathered fellowship.

Had I been any of our Lord's original disciples, I think
I would have chosen to be the one that voiced this royal
request, "Teach us to pray." This, indeed, is the soul's
grandest avenue into the presence of God.

Dr. Fosdick has pointed out that it is the only thing
on record Jesus was ever asked to teach them to do.

No one ever requested guidance in preaching or teaching
or help in any other area of Christian ministry. One thing
was felt to be needful.

The pertinent point that we wish to dwell on here, however, is the fact that this disciple came to Jesus with his earnest desire. He did not go to the Temple or the synagogue or to any of the religious guides of the Jewish faith. Why, in fact, did he present this sincere wish at the feet of our Lord?

I

This man came to Jesus because I think our Lord had *a time for prayer.*

The Gospel of Mark reveals that "he was up long before daybreak" (Mark 1:35, TLB). Now I certainly cannot prove that this was Jesus' habitual period for communion with the Father, but I think it was. Speaking from my own experience, I know there is a difference in my day when I begin it earnestly seeking his presence and guidance.

This was the conviction of another and he penned these words:

> I met God in the morning
>   When the day was at its best,
> And His Presence came like sunrise,
>   Like glory in my breast.
>
> All day long the presence lingered,
>   All day long he stayed with me,
> And we sailed in perfect calmness
>   O'er a very troubled sea.
>
> Other ships were blown and battered,
>   Other ships were sore distressed,
> But the winds that seemed to drive them,
>   Brought to us a peace and rest.
>
> Then I thought of other mornings,
>   With a keen remorse of mind,
> When I too had loosed the moorings,
>   With the Presence left behind.
>
> So, I think I know the secret,

Learned from many a troubled way:
You must seek him in the morning
If you want him through the day.[1]

Some years ago in our city, a certain church was planning a revival meeting. The decision was made to sponsor a twenty-four hour prayer vigil from Saturday evening to Sunday evening, when the services would offically begin.

There was a good response and each hour found several people promising to participate. At last every period had been signed for with the lone exception of one early morning hour.

At length, a young bank teller rather reluctantly wrote his name down in the final empty space.

"I favor the vigil," he chuckled, "but I had not planned to get up this early."

That has been quite a while ago and now as an influential executive he still keeps his rendezvous with the Lord early, and I mean every morning.

"I found," he said, that this was my only quiet time—away from phones and noise and distractions. I would not miss for anything this hour with Christ."

The disciples saw in Jesus that which was so like God and they wanted it. If our Lord did not have morning time with his Father, he did have some time. Don't miss your prayer tryst: morning, noon, evening, night. Nothing can replace it.

II

Then, I think that this disciple came to Jesus because our Lord had *a place for prayer*. "He was praying in a certain place."

---

[1] Ralph S. Cushman, "The Secret" from *Spiritual Hilltops* (New York: Abingdon-Cokesbury, 1932).

Now this is not to say that the world cannot be your prayer parish. One can pray anywhere, indeed everywhere. But it is to plead for a particular locality where the King's guest is welcomed into the King's presence.

Dr. Frank Boreham reminded us that Judas not only betrayed Jesus but that he betrayed his place of prayer. No spot is more sacred. No place is more needed.

I have a place. Sometimes I can come into my house when the day has been difficult and that very place will remind me where Christ has met me in times past. I have gone there with my joy and he has shared it. I have gone there with my emptiness and he has filled it. I have gone there with my grief and he has borne it. I have gone there with my surrender and he has blessed it.

I heard once of a farmer who had two sons. His wife, who was a Christian, had died and he was making the effort to guide these young men in the way everlasting.

Each morning just prior to doing the day's chores, the boys noticed that their father disappeared. They wondered about his absence but during his life never learned the secret of his withdrawal.

One day, months after his death, they were at work in the barn. Suddenly one of them discovered a cavity in the rear of the barn. He thought the space was completely filled with hay. Then he made another discovery. On a bale in the corner was an open Bible. In front of it were two worn-out places on the ground; places it had taken a long time to depress.

He called for his brother, and they stood in reverent silence before this scene of holiness. At length, one of them said, "So that's where he was and what he was doing." The other answered, "I'm just wondering how many of those prayers were said for us." Then one lad knelt in a knee print and the second knelt in the other. And when they got up, they rose with their father's God in their hearts.

Do you have a place? Will you find one?

III

There is a third reason and it is an urgent one. Jesus had *a power in prayer.* Here was his great soul strength: "Not my will, but thine, be done" (Luke 22:42, KJV).

Although these words are only found in connection with his Gethsemane passion, they were really the faith-foundation of his entire life. Listen to his words in similar vein: "He that hath seen me hath seen the Father" (John 14:9). That is not shallow surrender—that is the deepest dedication!

There is an old story with which, I am sure, most of us can easily identify.

A lady, passing a Methodist parsonage, observed the minister's son playing in the front yard.

"What is your father doing this morning?" she asked.

"Oh!" was the response, "the bishop has offered him a bigger appointment and he is praying about whether or not he should accept."

"That is interesting," she answered, "what is your mother doing?"

"Packing," was his immediate reply.

And I must confess that all too often that has been my procedure. "Not thy will, but mine be done." How often has that hindered my commitment and contribution.

But it doesn't have to be that way. I have a close friend in the ministry who is slowly dying of an incurable disease. Recently I was visiting him, and he had just returned from seeing his physician. When I asked if there was any hopeful news, he only shook his head. I sat there thinking of this sincere follower of our Lord, not yet forty—a lovely wife and three boys—and how he wants to preach.

"Jim," I blurted out, "how do you pray about it?"

He looked at me and fairly beamed. "Wallace," he answered, "there is just one prayer I can pray. Not my will, but thine, be done!"

In a way, he was wrong. I can think of several other prayers, any one of which I might very well have prayed.

"Lord, let me recover or I will quit the ministry."

"Father, let me get well or I will drop out of the church."

"Lord, heal me or I will turn sour."

But there was just one prayer this young Galahad of Gethsemane could pray. And, oh! The gold it is bringing into the treasure house of the hearts of the people who know him.

IV

Finally, I think the royal request, "Teach us to pray," was presented to Jesus because our Lord had *a victory in prayer.*

I am sure that the one making this request, as well as the other disciples, had seen what God's power had done in their Lord's life. They knew something of the burden he was bearing and when he would return from his place, it was obvious what his prayer pilgrimage had meant.

Some of them had witnessed his arrest. Peter had followed to the high priest's house. John had stood at the foot of the cross. It must have amazed them that there was not even the hint of frustration or fear. In fact, if one follows closely his arrest, trial, agony at death, he is convinced that Jesus seems to be the complete master of the situation.

There is but one reason for this astounding triumph. Our Lord harbored no doubt at Calvary because of his dedication in Gethsemane.

And here is the mighty climax of his victorious prayer

life. His final words are a prayer: "Father, into thy hands I commend my spirit." Now that is entering the gates with your flags flying and your banners streaming.

And his victory makes it possible for us to be victorious. Had he not said, "Be of good cheer; I have overcome the world" (John 16:33)?

A few Easters back we were sharing our family devotional. The topic we were discussing was "What Easter means," and I was asking each member of our home what it meant to them.

I shall never forget how my older son, then ten years old, responded. "Daddy," he said, "to me Easter means when he came alive, we come alive too!"

Yes, thank God! And eternally!

8
Christ and His Church

I say also unto thee, That thou art Peter, and upon this
rock I will build my church; and the gates of hell shall
not prevail against it (Matt. 16:18).

Not only do I consider it difficult for one to grow spiri-
tually outside the church, the body of Christ, I think it
is impossible.

It is my feeling that if one is to mature as a practicing
follower of our Lord he must share at least three experiences.

First, there is the experience of one's own devotional
conduct. Second, there is the experience of the small group
meeting. This, too, is one of the rich fruits of the lay witness
mission. Third, there is the experience of a dynamic worship
service as part of the gathered fellowship.

Now, I consider these imperative and they are all a
definite part of the church, for mark you, the church is
always where God and man meet.

Look again at the three things we have mentioned.

We suggested that the church sustains the devotional
life of each person. That is to say it is not program but

prayer. The church is the small group fellowship. Dr. Trueblood is quite correct when he affirms that Jesus did not so much save the world as he trained eleven disciples to save it. So the church is not primarily a sanctuary but a sharing. And the church is a victorious celebration as people meet together in divine worship. But again it is not essentially a building but a brotherhood.

So! Christ's body functions through a personal, a preparing, a public witness to his grace.

With this in mind, let us examine, in the light of Jesus' own words, what he had to say about the church.

I

Jesus said, "I will build my church," that is, *the church is of God.* And because it is his, this means the doors are open to everyone. In the words of another, the doors of the church are as wide as the gates of heaven.

Let me say, in the first place, the church is for every *color.* Sometimes it is interesting to note the response when you observe that Jesus was not, in fact, a white man. I have visited the homeland of our Lord and his people are brown skinned people.

Sometime ago I was engaged in conversation with a man from about the deepest section of our southland although he now lives farther north.

"I feel," he suggested, "that the nigger [and I thought I saw what was coming by the use of this term] is about two steps up from a baboon." I sat still wondering how I would answer when he continued, "I will say this, however. On our plantation there was an old black mammy. Until I was practically grown, every bite of food I ate, she cooked, and every stitch of clothing I wore, she made. When she died, I drove hundreds of miles to attend her funeral."

I said, "My friend, that is a very long way to go to bury a baboon, isn't it?" He got the point and somehow I believe it made a difference.

Jesus said, "Him that cometh to me I will in no wise cast out." And thank God! That means the black, the white, the red, the yellow, the brown. It means every *him* in the world.

Then, because the church is of God, it is for every *class.* Often, I fear that some of us would be as wary of a poverty clad person as a different colored skin. It is just as wrong to be class prejudiced as color prejudiced and, perhaps in our affluent age, worse.

I am glad when I remember that my denomination, the United Methodist Church, started on the Oxford campus under Wesley. But I need also to reflect upon the fact that a man named George Whitefield had a great deal to do with the spread of Methodist thinking. And his people operated a saloon.

Do you recall those words inscribed on the tablet of the Statue of Liberty?

> Give me your tired, your poor,
>   Your huddled masses yearning to breathe free,
> The wretched refuse of your teeming shore.
>   Send these, the homeless, tempest-tost to me,
> I lift up my lamp beside the golden door.
> *—Emma Lazarus*

This is the church's responsibility. But more—it is its privilege.

The church, the body of Christ, is for every *creed.* Some words of the apostle Paul are significant here. "Our bodies have many parts, but the many parts make up only one body when they are all put together. So it is with the 'body' of Christ. Each of us is a part of the one body of Christ.

Some of us are Jews, some are Gentiles. . . . But the Holy Spirit has fitted us all together into one body" (1 Cor. 12:12-13, TLB).

I served a church once where we had boiler trouble just before the hour of worship. Our Jewish friends, just a few blocks away, opened the doors of their synagogue to us with warmth and welcome. It was the beginning of a harmonious relationship which still exists.

As I understand it, the real tragedy in our country is not so much the Jew who makes no profession of Christ as Savior, but indifferent members of Christ's several churches who profess without practicing the faith.

And I like very much a statement from Sam Jones. "When I am asked," he said, "why I do not preach more against the Catholics, my answer is, 'When I get through with the Methodists, its bedtime!' "

The last thing we want to say at this point is that the church is for every *condition*. Jesus advised that this was the reason for the incarnation. Listen again to his words: "The Son of man is come to seek and to save that which was lost" (Luke 19:10).

When one gets right down to it, there are just two kinds of people in the world. Not the black and the white—there are other colors. Not the rich and the poor—there are many in-betweeners. Not the intelligent and the ignorant—there are many who have some measure of education. There are the saved and lost.

It is to these who do not walk in the light of his way that those of us who belong to his body must offer the most winsome friendship and the most glorious tidings.

Make no mistake about it—winning people for his kingdom may not be the only business of the church, but it is the supreme business of the church. If people, young and old, are not finding God in the church, then it really does not matter how many buildings we are erecting or how large a budget we are raising or what kind of program we are presenting. Unless, and until, people of all colors and classes and creeds and conditions are walking through the gates of new life, then the church is helpless in its ministry to the world and we are leaving Christ forsaken on a lonely hill.

II

Jesus said, "Upon this rock," and this tells us *the church is of faith*. When Jesus used this phrase, he was responding to Peter's confident affirmation, "Thou art the Christ." And it is only upon this confession, the rock-like assertion that Jesus is, in fact, the Savior that the fellowship of his followers can be solidly established.

Do you recall that memorable occasion during the Feast of Tabernacles when our Lord's true character was being discussed? There seemed to be three opinions.

One group suggested, "He is a good man" (John 7:12). Another company responded by saying, "He deceiveth the people" (John 7:12). But there were others who asked, "Do the rulers know indeed that this is the very Christ?" (John 7:26). And again we read in that same setting, "Many of the people believed on him, and said, When Christ cometh, will he do more miracles than these which this man hath done?" (John 7:31).

So they had these three alternatives from which to choose. He was simply a man or he was a deceiver or he is the Christ. I submit they are the choices that lie before us today. With all my heart I urge that we claim him as the Christ, the Savior of the world.

I was interested in a discussion two young people were having on a certain college campus here in my city.

The girl said, in effect, "I do not think highly of the

term 'Savior.' That turns me off. I prefer the word, 'identify.' This speaks to me in a much better way."

The boy answered, "But if you were in a burning building, would you want the firemen to identify with you or save you?" And that ended the conversation.

When we say, "You are the Christ—the Savior," it enables him to say, "You are the rock." And thank God! It is on this commitment that his church can be built.

III

Jesus said, "the gates of hell shall not prevail against it," and this reminds us that *the church is of eternity.*

Other translations make this line read, "the powers of death shall not prevail against it."

Both are meaningful and positive. Death and hell cannot stand in the way of the body of Christ—the fellowship of the faith—the church!

Think once more of Jesus' significant words to his disciples:

"Go ye therefore, and teach all nations, baptizing them in the name of the Father, and the Son, and of the Holy Ghost: Teaching them to observe all things whatsoever I have commanded you: and, lo, I am with you alway, even unto the end of the world" (Matt. 28:19-20).

We can do *for* him because he has promised to be *with* us.

Or to put it differently, in the Gospel of John we read his words, "because I live, you shall live also" (John 14:19, RSV).

It is the living Lord who gives to the world a living church. The gates of hell—the powers of death shall not prevail against it.

Not long ago, I was marrying a young couple in one of our neighborhood churches in Nashville.

Just before the ceremony, Jeanne whispered, "Mr. Chappell, could you make a change in the ritual?"

I said, "I am not sure, Jeanne. Being a Methodist, I try to uphold its rituals. What did you have in mind?"

"Well," she answered, "after a weekend honeymoon, Bob goes back to Vietnam. Instead of saying, 'til death us do part,' could you say 'forever and ever'?"

If a young sailor boy and a lovely college co-ed could affirm that kind of faith to each other, would you think the Lord Jesus would promise less to his followers?

"I am with you always." Always is the promise. The "I" and "you" are the church.

V.

THE TASK

9.
The Measure of Greatness

Your care for others is the measure of your greatness (Luke
9:48, TLB).

We have looked at the need and the call and the gift
and the growth. We turn now to the task.

At the time that these words were spoken by Jesus in
Luke's Gospel, an argument had just taken place among
the disciples as to who was greatest.

There follows then that memorable scene where our Lord
placed a child in their midst and talked to them about
concern instead of world-labeled greatness. The climax is
found in this sentence: Your care for others is the measure
of your greatness.

This is our task! All else that has to do with the kingdom
depends on whether or not we care and how deeply.

Von Hugel was right when he affirmed that caring is
everything. And Saint John of the Cross expressed it in
these words: "Finally, judgment will ask only one question:
Did you love?"

It is imperative, too, that we understand that this loving,
this caring for others, is the mission of all who belong

to the body of Christ: minister and layman.

Here are two illustrations that I think speak to this fact.

I heard about a Catholic chaplain who, at the risk of his life, crawled many yards in a battle zone to minister to a wounded boy. "But Chaplain," the injured lad remonstrated, "I don't belong to your church." "No, son," came the answer, "but you belong to my Christ."

The other story involves a stenographer and a young Navy lad. During the war, he went to her business establishment for the purpose of talking to the office manager. He left moments later entirely different. But let him tell about it, himself, in a letter to that employer. (I am indebted to Dr. Paul Scherer for this story.)

DEAR SIR:

I'm a sailor an I'll be pulling out in a few hours, but first I've got something I want to say. I came into your office this morning lonely and scared to death about sailing again. I wanted to talk to somebody pretty bad. So when the girl at the desk said hello I went in and asked her if she had a job for me. She said for me to sit down for a few minutes so I did. I told her maybe there wouldn't be jobs or anything afterwards that if a fellow could only be sure something would come through, worth dying for it wouldn't be so bad. She smiled and said, "That's easy. Christ is coming through and he's worth dying for." I just looked at her and she talked as if he were alive and a good pal of hers. I sort of expected to see him walk in the door, it was so real.

I was only there for about ten minutes and I don't know why but her talking like that sort of did something to me and I'm not lonely anymore and I'm not scared. It was like she had said, "I want to make you acquainted with my friend, Jesus. You ought to get to know each other since he'll be going your way." I'm nineteen and I never knew before that there was a God like that who would go along with a fellow. It don't matter so much now if my ship goes down and I go down so long as there's a God that no sub can sink.

Here let us make five observations.

I

First, there are those who do not care at all.

The best illustration of this I know is when the broken-hearted Judas realized what he had done by betraying Jesus. Taking the thirty silver pieces back to the priests and elders, he confessed that he had done wrong. Listen to their heartless answer: "What do we care about that?" (Matt. 27:4, TEV).

And let me remind you that these were the spiritual advisors of Judas, the shepherds of his boyhood. If he could have received help from any source, it should have been there. But he did not get it.

I am thinking of a girl who came to see me one day. She had gone wrong and she knew it. She was seeking guidance from her minister. Her bad days are gone now. She is happily married and has a nice family. I think perhaps that God used me to give her hope during a crucial time. But I wonder what might have happened if I had said to her, "What do I care about that?"

Yet I wonder, too, if I have not neglected, many times by what I have or have not done, to offer comfort and courage to those who were passing through deep waters.

There are millions today whose lives are troubled and whose hours are desperate. It might be that just the knowledge of a person who cares could transform darkness into daybreak.

An old friend of mine used to say, "Sometimes a Christian only makes a little difference. But sometimes that little difference makes all the difference."

II

· Then there are those who care or seem to but only when being seen. Look, for instance, at those two great Christian affirmations, *giving* and *praying,* both of which should have others as one of their supreme considerations. Here is what Jesus had to say about them.

"When you give alms, sound no trumpet before you" (Matt. 6:2, RSV).

"When you pray, go into your room and shut the door" (Matt. 6:6, RSV). Evidently Jesus really meant business when he said, "Do not let your left hand know what your right hand is doing" (Matt. 6:3, RSV).

No doubt that poor widow had very few eyes upon her, and certainly her gift of two coins caused no trumpets to blow, but Jesus felt that the offering she brought was the supreme contribution that day in Jerusalem. The greatness of the story is not only that the gift was all she had but that it was not done for applause.

There was once a very dear farmer friend of mine who had great compassion for people. He was concerned especially when there had been accidents or sickness and the families were in need of financial assistance. He would send them money through the mail, but he always made it a habit to disguise his handwriting and cross the river so there would be a different postmark.

III

There are people who care, but only for their own.

It was Jesus' outreaching love, his beautiful offer of divine and human friendship for all people, that really was the new dimension in his messianic mission.

Certainly he came as Savior to the Jews, but we read that "In his own land and among his own people he was not accepted" (John 1:11-12, TLB). But then we read "to *all* who received him, he gave the right to become children of God."

So! That word "all" became the veritable theme of his tidings, and "the world" (John 3:16) the extension of his conquest.

Or to say it in a little different vein, here is a bit of sarcastic humor that I think has merit. It is a word of doggerel quoted by William Barclay in *Flesh and Spirit:*

> We are God's chosen few,
>   All others will be damned;
> There is no room in heaven for you—
>   We can't have heaven crammed.

The reason why I think Luke is the greatest of all the Gospels is because it is the good news for the whole wide world. Only in this Gospel do we read that "all flesh shall see the salvation of God" (Luke 3:6, RSV).

But we must not miss the elementary fact that not only is the gospel bigger than local church, wider than nationality, inclusive of each color, open to every condition; it is when self is committed that the door opens to these larger ministries.

I read about a young man who was serving a life sentence in a penitentiary. Like many of the other inmates his life was acquiring a bitterness and hardness that was deplorable. Life held no promise, and he was making no contribution. One day he discovered a paragraph in a newspaper that spoke to his heart. It was about another prisoner who had offered himself as a guinea pig to the Medical Corps and had subsequently died. He asked to see the warden. Granted the interview, he showed him the clipping and said, "Warden, I would love to do that."

The warden replied, "You mean you want to die?"

"No," was his answer. "I want a chance to come alive. I want to give myself for a cause that is bigger than I am."

IV

There are people who care, but only at particular times. Their emotions are pricked just at certain seasons. During Advent or Lent or perhaps at Pentecost, they feel the need to share in a ministry of love to people. It would seem, however, to the outsider that the rest of the year they could not care less.

And we should seriously consider this: These people who shun Christian fellowship are often quite thoughtful. They have manufactured excuses why they should abstain. Every now and then you look at one's defense that really seems justifiable. What is our answer, for instance, when someone says that two or three times a year we show a bit of concern and the remainder no interest, no love, no expression?

Look at Thomas. When Jesus felt constrained to go to Bethany, and that meant opposition, Thomas said, "Let us also go, that we may die with him" (John 11:16, RSV). But where was Thomas later when our Lord needed him so greatly?

Think of Peter. In the shadow of Calvary, he said to the Master, "I will lay down my life for you" (John 13:37, RSV). But when the hour of crucifixion had arrived, how conspicuous was the fisherman by his absence.

Last December, a businessman who had experienced genuine concern said a thing that is worthy of reflection. "I have decided," he commented, "to make Christmas and not buy it." And this is what we are talking about. Buying Christmas—that is a onetime gift. But making Christmas—that is lifetime service.

V

Finally, there are those who care all the time—who maintain a constant concern for others.

One of the great verses in the Bible is this: "Thou dost keep him in perfect peace, whose mind is stayed on thee, because he trusts in thee" (Isa. 26:3, RSV). And of course it is true. But I have found in the twenty five years that I have been in the ministry that it is also these God-kept people with the staying minds and the trusting hearts that care most for the needs of people.

Make no mistake about it—the one way we prove our love for God is by our love for others. And it is the most beautiful when it is the most lasting.

Here is what I am trying to say in the words of a poem that means a great deal to me.

> I sometimes think about the Cross,
> And shut my eyes and try to see
> The cruel nails and crown of thorns,
> And Jesus crucified for me.
>
> But even could I see him die,
> I could but see a little part
> Of that great love which like a fire
> Is always burning in His heart.
> —*Leslie Weatherhead*

You see, Christ's cross is *always* because Christ's love is *always*.

I read of an experience which a man shared that moved me deeply.

One cold rainy night while he was waiting at a bus stop, an elderly woman got off a bus and stood beside him. "Can you tell me when the next bus is due?" she asked. When the man asked which bus she wanted, she answered his query. "But you just got off that one," he observed. "Well," she stammered a bit shyly, "you see, there was a terribly crippled man on that bus and nobody offered him a seat. I knew he would be embarrassed if an old lady like me got up for him, so I just pretended it was time for me to get off. I rang the bell just as he was standing by my seat. He wasn't embarrassed and I—well, there is always another bus."

If a person acts like that, it is because the person lives like that. They have in their hearts the permanent disposition of Jesus Christ.

10.
Why People Listened to Jesus

David therefore himself calleth him Lord; and whence is
he then the son? And the common people heard him gladly
(Mark 12:37).

How can we rightly share Jesus' love without realizing
how he himself shared that love?

The common people heard him gladly. And let me say
at this point, no one is breaking down doors at either our
church or home to hear my witness. Probably you are not
having this difficulty either.

Why don't they hear us gladly?

One reason may be that people are not certain we, as
Christians, know the Way.

I was driving with a layman sometime ago who made
a most discerning observation.

"What is the one thing you expect of your minister?"
was my question.

"To convince me that he's convinced," was the answer.

Still another reason that we are not heard gladly may
be that we do not speak from vital association with the
Scriptures. Sometimes when I am in missions, especially

with the Scottish and English ministers, I am aware of how the crowds flock to their interpretation of the Word.

A member of a certain minister's congregation said, "I heard you preach this morning and if that text had had smallpox the sermon never would have caught it." I rather doubt that he was being complimentary.

Then, it is a distinct possibility that people do not hear our tidings gladly because we straddle the fence. "Stay off the median," should not only be seen on our Interstate Highways but also in our pulpits and places of witness everywhere.

Once a newspaper carried an editorial about a particular politician. The closing sentence is something to think about. "Thus he stands," it read, "as he always does, on both sides of the issue."

One simply can not do that and companion with our Lord or champion his cause.

I will mention a final factor. It may be the biggest reason of all.

The common people may not hear us gladly because there is a discrepancy between our talking and our living.

I shall never forget what a young minister in our seminary said. "We tell each other dirty jokes," he observed. "Sometimes we tell our church members these trashy jokes too. One day we will stand in the pulpit and preach on, 'Blessed are the pure in heart for they shall see God,' and they will think that is a joke too."

What an indictment!

Now let us come to the main question before us. Why did the common people hear our blessed Lord gladly?

I

The first reason, I think, the common people heard Jesus gladly was because he was glad.

Never do we read in the New Testament that Jesus laughed. Yet, we know that he took the little children in his arms and blessed them. I find it difficult to believe that these little ones would have left their parents' care pursuing the friendship of one whose face was not radiant and whose countenance was not joyous.

Two years before he increased the temperature of heaven by his entrance, Dr. E. Stanley Jones preached in our pulpit. I remember many points he made, but one in particular can never be forgotten. The great missionary said, "When I was seventeen, I thought I was having a lot of fun with Jesus. When I was twenty-seven and thirty-seven and forty-seven and fifty-seven and sixty-seven and seventy-seven I thought I was having a lot of fun with Jesus. Now I'm eighty-seven and its getting funnier all the time." And the glow on his face proved the words he had spoken were true.

Jesus made God so real and life so glad that to be in his presence was to live in the fullness of joy.

Even the Temple police who were not known as his friends spoke these words concerning him: "He says such wonderful things! We've never heard anything like it" (John 7:46, TLB).

And he himself said, "My purpose is to give life in all its fullness" (John 10:10, TLB). What could make for more gladness than that?

II

Then I feel that the common people heard Jesus gladly because they understood him.

Listen to some of his words that still bring millions comfort and joy.

"Come unto me, all ye that labour and are heavy laden, and I will give you rest" (Matt. 11:28).

"Thy faith hath made thee whole; go in peace" (Mark 5:34).

"Him that cometh to me I will in no wise cast out" (John 6:37).

It would be rather difficult not to know the meaning of these simple but significant truths.

It is interesting to go through the Scriptures and count the one syllable words Jesus used. Take, for instance, that second selection that we just used from the Gospel of Mark. Every word in that great sentence is a word of a single syllable.

Simplicity is a great need for our day, as we seek to share the message of Christ with a partially pagan civilization.

One could learn much from the simple sharing of Philip with his new Ethiopian friend in that long-ago desert scene. Here is an unforgettable line that never ceases to convict my superfluity: "Philip opened his mouth . . . and preached unto him Jesus" (Acts 8:35).

Dr. Fosdick once said that he could understand every word Paul Tillich said but not a single sentence. How marvelous that words and sentences from the Galilean can be understood by even a child.

My daughter, Cathy, was eight years old when we saw and heard Billy Graham on television one night years ago. I remember being rather amazed that she seemed so attentive. Turning cartwheels or scrapping with her little brother would have offered no surprise. But as Mr. Graham told of Jesus and the blind man that was healed in the beautiful simplicity of the Gospel account, her interest could not have been more genuine.

We read in Luke this simple climax to the story: "The man followed Jesus" (Luke 18:43, TLB). And so did Cathy

III

I would suggest that, in the third place, the common people heard Jesus gladly because he was one of them.

This was primarily the reason he chose to be baptized. I was baptized because I had a past to confess. He did have a future to consecrate. But the main reason he was baptized of John was so that he could say to the people, "I choose to be identified with you—I am one of you."

It reminds us of Ezekiel and his ministry to the people of his day. Do you recall his words: "I sat where they sat" (Ezek. 3:15)?

We must learn that we can never reach persons for the Master until, like the Samaritan in Jesus' parable, we are willing to go where they are and, regardless of any inconvenience, rescue them.

It was said of the great scholar and saint, Henry Drummond, that often he could be seen walking the streets late at night with his arm around some neglected drunkard telling him about a love that could set him free. No wonder his students clung to his words and drank from his fountain. The classic illustration, I think, is that of Dr. Ernest Freemont Tittle. Some men were discussing his social emphases. There were both positive and negative comments expressed. One layman admitted that he did not agree with all of Tittle's social sermons and theories and pronouncements. "But," he said in words something like these, "when my wife died, and I was considering suicide, he came and walked with me through the shadows. He made the difference for me between life and death. No, I don't concur with all he says. However, it is his practice outside the pulpit that makes me endorse his preaching inside the pulpit."

My favorite translator, Dr. William Barclay, says that the incarnation means God got with us.

And, of course, he did—in Christ! I take it, then, because of his grace and love and joy we, in turn, are to get with others.

IV

The biggest reason, however, that I think the common people heard Jesus gladly was because they did not feel common after they heard him share the truth of God.

I know that the word "common" referred more to crowd than class, and yet it was basically the ordinary man that Jesus appealed to the most. He was not in the strictest sense a scribe or a sage or scholar. He was a carpenter and he made his greatest inroads in the lives of the men of the streets. Once more, this is the major ministry of the lay witness mission.

When the common man heard that voice and felt that tug and shared that grace, he knew what Isaiah had meant centuries before when he announced that "they shall mount up with wings as eagles" (Isa. 40:31).

I heard my old professor, Ray Jordan, use an illustration that I think reveals the truth of this point.

Robert Burns and some of his friends were dining in a Scottish inn. The tavern boy, as he approached their table with drinks and food, slipped and fell on the floor. Goblets, utensils, and food went in all directions. The innkeeper came in—cuffed the boy, cursed him, and fired him.

As the lad walked out, quite dejected, Burns followed him. Putting his arm around the boy, he said to him, "You can be somebody."

And Sir Walter Scott never got over that. Years later when he was giving the world his "Lady of the Lake

Date Due

and "Ivanhoe," he said, "The greatest lift I ever got was when Bobbie Burns told me I could be somebody."

Someone greater than the poet of Scotland addresses our hearts. It is the Christ of God who speaks to us and bids us rise.

About the Author

Dr. Wallace Davis Chappell is the senior minister of the McKendree United Methodist Church, Nashville, Tennessee. This church in the heart of downtown Nashville is rich in historical significance, having served faithfully since 1787. The church is noted for its warm fellowship and dynamic evangelism.

Dr. Chappell is a native of Asheville, North Carolina. He is married to the former Mary Frances Whitenack. The Chappells have three children, Catherine, Wallace Davis, and Richard Kent. Dr. Chappell is the nephew of the late Dr. Clovis Chappell, one of Methodism's greats.

Before coming to McKendree church, Chappell served as pastor of the Nolachuckey Circuit, Holston Conference (1956-1959) and then as pastor of three Nashville churches: Buchanan Street (1959-1963), Woodbine (1963-1966), and Blakemore (1966-1969).

He is a graduate of Emory Henry College, Birmingham Southern College, and Emory University. Trevecca Nazarene College honored him with the D.D.

He won a Civitan Club award as "Minister of the Year" in 1972. He is in demand for conferences and special meetings throughout the nation. His first Broadman book was *When Jesus Rose*. He has done five books with other publishers.